The Complete Electric Bass Method

Beginning · Intermediate · Mastering

DAVID OVERTHROW

Alfred, the leader in educational publishing, and the National Guitar Workshop, one of America's finest guitar schools, have joined forces to bring you the best, most progressive educational tools possible. We hope you will enjoy this book and encourage you to look for other fine products from Alfred and the National Guitar Workshop.

ISBN 0-7390-0682-7 Book
ISBN 0-7390-0683-5 Book and CD

This book was acquired, edited and produced
by Workshop Arts, Inc., the publishing arm of the National Guitar Workshop.

Nathaniel Gunod, editor
Joe Bouchard, music typesetter
Timothy Phelps, interior book design
The CD was recorded at Bar None Studios, Northford, CT

Cover photograph: Karen Miller

TABLE OF CONTENTS

Track 1

A compact disc is available with each book of this series. Using these discs will help make learning more enjoyable and the information more meaningful. Each disc features an entire rhythm section playing most of the examples. It is important for you to play along with the CD as much as possible. This disc features some great players so, in effect, you can play with great players without leaving your home. The CD helps you play the correct notes, rhythms and feel of each example. The track numbers below the symbols correspond directly to the example you want to hear. Track 1 will help you tune to this CD. Have fun!

ABOUT THE AUTHOR

PHOTO · STUART RABINOWITZ

Dave Overthrow has been a bass performer and instructor for over 20 years. He studied at Berklee College of Music and later earned a Bachelor of Music degree from Western Connecticut State University. Dave was a member of the bass faculty at the National Guitar Summer Workshop for ten years, from its beginning in 1984 until 1994. He is presently Director of Music and Head of Jazz Studies at the Canterbury School in New Milford, Connecticut. Dave performs regularly in New York City and Connecticut. In addition to appearing on several CDs in styles ranging from funk to rock to reggae, Dave records with his own band, HIPpOCKET.

INTRODUCTION

Welcome to the third book of a three-book series about creating bass lines. The format of this book is similar to *Beginning Electric Bass* and *Intermediate Electric Bass* in that it helps you learn how to create your own bass lines from a set of given chord changes. Like other books, this book gives you plenty of great bass lines to play, but more importantly, this book gives you the tools to help you learn how to construct your own bass lines in different styles.

To get the most out of this book, you should already be familiar with the material covered in *Beginning Electric Bass* and *Intermediate Electric Bass*. You should know triads, 7 chords, diatonic harmony, major scales, the modes of the major scale, diatonic passing tones, chromatic passing tones and minor scales. A firm grasp of these concepts will allow you to learn the new material more easily.

This series contains an enormous amount of material. It would be helpful to supplement this information with lessons, practice and other instructional books, such as *Building Bass Lines* by Chuck Archer, to further your development as a player. And, of course, playing with other musicians is perhaps the most important educational thing you can do.

This method is designed to help you create bass lines from the simple to the complex. Although *Mastering Electric Bass* is more advanced, *Beginning Electric Bass* and *Intermediate Electric Bass* contain vital information for any bassist. Ideally, every bassist should learn about the building blocks of bass lines and learn chord structures thoroughly—*Beginning Electric Bass* discusses this in detail. *Intermediate Electric Bass* helps the bassist learn how common scale forms are used in bass lines in different styles of bass playing. Even experienced players would benefit from checking out these books. All three books work well as an organized method to be used on your own or with an instructor.

I hope you have a good time while playing the bass lines and encourage you to absorb this information and apply it to your own playing situations. Have fun!

DEDICATION
This book is dedicated to my family, especially my mother, Shirley Rose, and my brother Keith Overthrow, who have continued to support me through all of my musical endeavors. This book is also dedicated to the many students I have taught, both privately and at the Canterbury School. They have helped make my teaching a fun learning experience. Also, thanks to Yvette for her never ending patience.

ACKNOWLEDGMENTS
Thanks to: the people at the National Guitar Workshop—especially Dave Smolover, Nat Gunod and Joe Bouchard; Ron Blake for the amazing basses he built for me; Tom Sheehy and J.P. Mandler at Canterbury School for allowing the music program to expand; Chris Morrison and Kurt Berglund who played on the CD that accompanies this series of books. I would also like to thank Al Street and Bruce Tibbitts for their contributions to the CD.

CHAPTER 1

Review

This chapter will review some of the concepts that were discussed in *Intermediate Electric Bass*. It is best that the main points of that book are fresh in your mind before you begin to study new material. Some of the scales are reviewed in this chapter with fingerings and sample bass lines, but check out *Intermediate Electric Bass* if you haven't already. It offers many more bass lines using the scales in this chapter. Have fun!

CIRCLE OF 5THS

As you progress through this book, you will encounter bass lines in many different keys and the *circle of 5ths* is a systematic way for you to become familiar with these keys. The circle of 5ths is a clockwise arrangement of successive keys, in order of ascending perfect 5ths.

In the circle of 5ths, each successive key introduces an additional sharp until the flat keys are reached, and then each new key has one less flat. The circle takes you through all twelve keys. This circle is also commonly called the *cycle of 5ths*. Also, many musicians think of it as a *cycle of 4ths*, which is just a counter-clockwise view of the circle. When you move through counter-clockwise, the intervals are all 4ths. This would take you through the flat keys first.

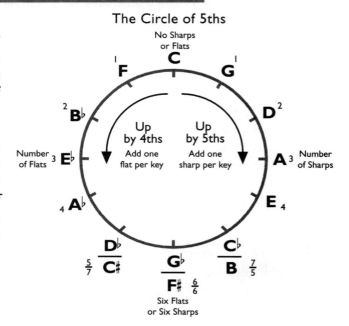

The Circle of 5ths

MAJOR PENTATONIC SCALE

The major pentatonic scale includes the tonic (1), 2, 3, 5 and 6 of the major scale.

C MAJOR PENTATONIC

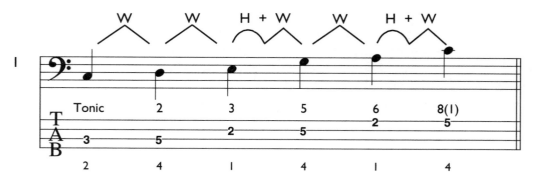

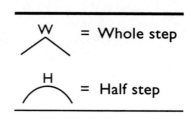

W = Whole step

H = Half step

MAJOR PENTATONIC SCALE FINGERINGS

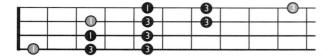

#1   #2

Two-Octave Fingering

The major pentatonic scale is commonly found in rock, country-rock and country, as well as other styles of music. It has a happy, light-hearted sound.

Geddy Lee has been a major creative force behind Rush, a Canadian rock group that released their first album in 1974. He has contributed vocals and synthesizers to Rush's sound, and his bass lines are some of the most innovative and creative in rock.

TEMPO INDICATIONS

The *tempo* (speed) for each example and piece in this book is shown with a *metronome marking*. For example, ♩ = 88 means to set your metronome to 88. Each click represents one beat. Play at the speed of the clicks.

MAJOR PENTATONIC BASS LINES

MINOR PENTATONIC SCALE

The minor pentatonic scale includes the 1, ♭3, 4, 5 and ♭7 of a major scale. These scale degrees can be achieved by either altering the major scale or thinking of the tonic, 3rd, 4th, 5th and 7th degrees of a natural minor scale. The natural minor scale is the same as the Aeolian mode, which is reviewed on pages 13 and 15. Also see page 89 of *Intermediate Electric Bass*.

C MINOR PENTATONIC

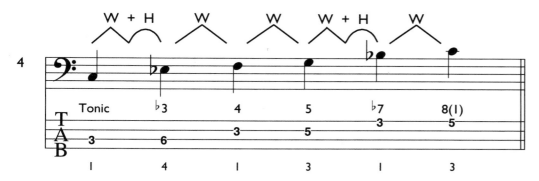

MINOR PENTATONIC SCALE FINGERINGS

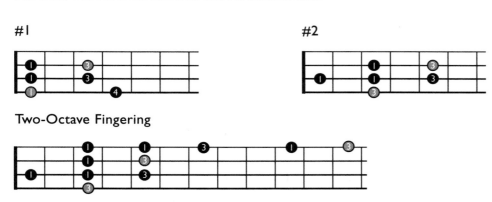

The minor pentatonic scale is indispensable for most styles of rock music, but is also commonly found in blues and other styles of music. Because of the minor 3rd (♭3), the minor pentatonic scale has a sad or melancholy feeling.

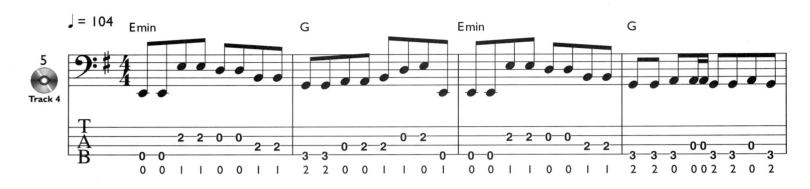

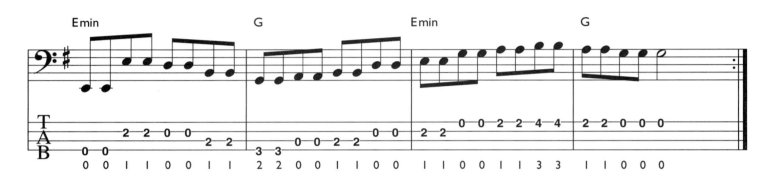

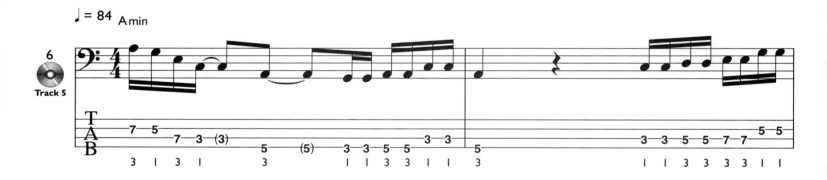

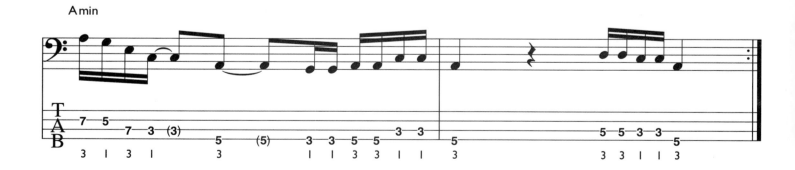

BLUES SCALE

When the ♭5 tone is added to the minor pentatonic scale, the result is the blues scale. The scale includes the 1, ♭3, 4, ♭5, 5 and ♭7 of a major scale.

C BLUES SCALE

BLUES SCALE FINGERINGS

#1   #2

Two-Octave Fingering

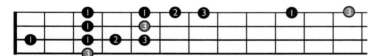

The blues scale is primarily used in blues music, but since the blues is the basis for both jazz and rock, it is an important part of the musical vocabularies of those styles.

BLUES SCALE LICKS

These are rock-style licks using the blues scale. There are lots of sixteenth notes, so don't try to play these until you are warmed up. Start slowly and work up to the suggested tempos.

MODES OF THE MAJOR SCALE

RELATIVE THINKING

The major scale can be thought of as containing seven modes. For example, if you play the C Major scale starting and ending on D, the 2nd degree, you have played the second mode, which is called the Dorian mode. If you start on E and end on E, you have played the third mode, which is called the Phrygian mode.

Here are the modes of the major scale in the key of C. Notice that the half steps (shown in grey boxes) are located between different scale degrees in each mode. This is what gives each mode its unique sound.

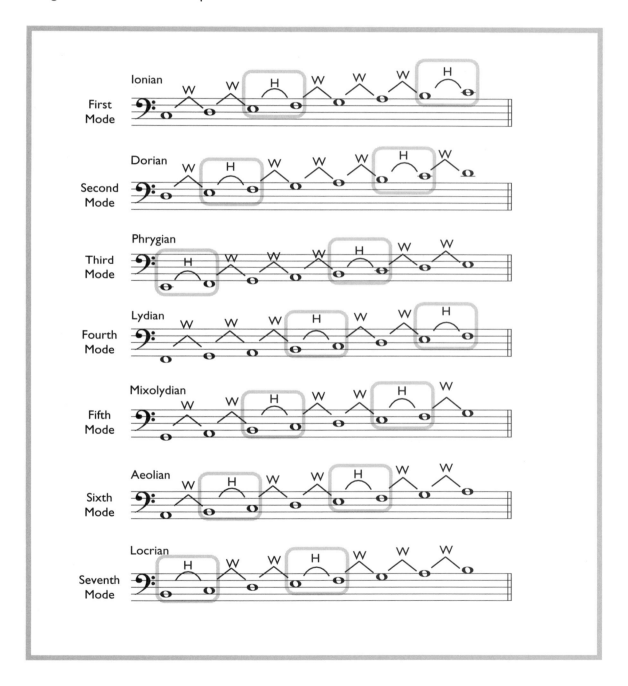

PARALLEL THINKING

Below, all seven modes of the major scale are built on the note C. These modes are now not diatonic to the key of C, but rather, they are *parallel* to C. With all of the modes built on the note C, it is easy to see the notes that are different from the major scale, and, therefore, characteristic to each mode. The notes that are changed from their positions in the C Major scale are marked (♭3, ♭7, etc.) To review the different fingerings for each of these modes, refer to *Intermediate Electric Bass*, page 45.

Below are all seven modes built on C. When you play these, listen to the characteristic sound of each.

IONIAN (SAME AS THE MAJOR SCALE)

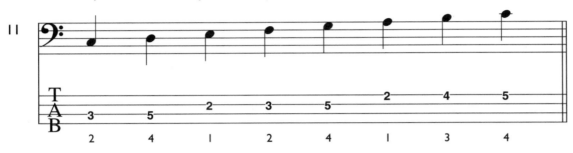

DORIAN

PHRYGIAN

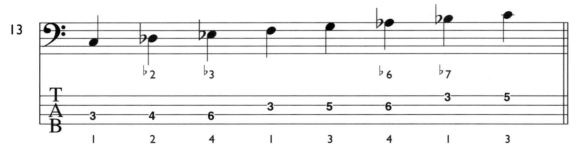

LYDIAN

MIXOLYDIAN

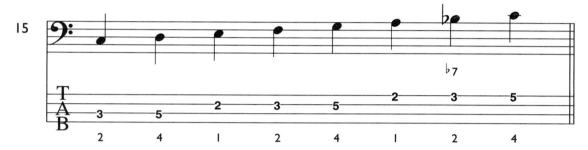

AEOLIAN (SAME AS THE NATURAL MINOR SCALE)

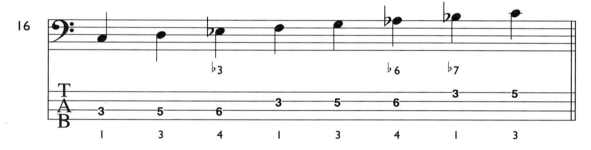

LOCRIAN

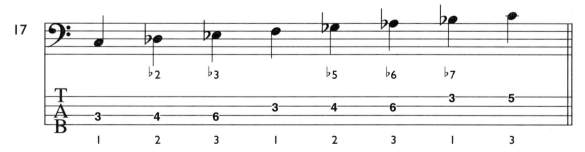

SLAP & POP NOTATION

A variety of different symbols are used to indicate the different elements of slap & pop technique in standard music notation and TAB. The following Key shows you the symbols for the techniques used in this book, followed by an explanation of the basics of each technique.

KEY

S	=	Slap	P0	=	Pull-off
P	=	Pop	×	=	Dead note
H	=	Hammer-on			

SLAP & POP TECHNIQUES

SLAP
Use the heel of the right thumb to strike the string. Let the thumb bounce off of the string so that you don't stop the string from ringing.

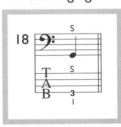 

POP
Place the right-hand 1st finger ⊓ slightly underneath the string (usually the 1st or 2nd) and pull it up hard enough so that it will "snap" back down against the frets.

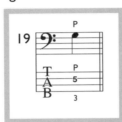 

HAMMER-ON
A hammer-on is executed by tapping the string with a left-hand finger to sound a higher pitched note without plucking with the right hand. For example, play the D on the 5th fret of the 3rd string with the 1st finger of the left hand. Now, tap the string on the 7th fret with the 3rd finger. Do this with enough force to cause the E on the 7th fret to sound without using the right hand at all.

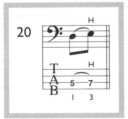

PULL-OFF
A pull-off is executed by snapping a left-hand finger off of a string in such a way as to cause a lower pitched note to sound without plucking with the right hand. For example, play the E on the 7th fret of the 3rd string while also holding the 1st finger on the 5th fret D. Now pull the 3rd finger away from the string (snap it—don't just pick it up) with enough force to cause the D on the 5th fret to sound without using the right hand at all.

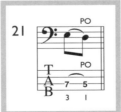

Pull-offs very often follow hammer-ons. Try the hammer-on described in example 20 and immediately follow it with the pull-off in example 21. Pluck the string only once, but play three notes (pluck, hammer-on, pull-off).

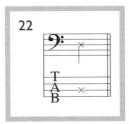

DIATONIC PASSING TONES AND CHORD SCALES

Bass lines are often made up of both chord tones and non-chord tones. The next few pages briefly discuss non-chord tones commonly used in many styles of music.

A *passing tone* connects chord tones in a stepwise manner. This allows for smooth, linear bass lines. A *diatonic passing tone* is a note from the scale of the key. So, if you are playing a bass line for a tune in C Major and use tones that are from the C Major scale, you will either be playing chord tones or diatonic passing tones to move from chord tone to chord tone smoothly.

You can also use passing tones from the scale that fits with the chord of that moment which is sometimes called a *chord scale*. Modes are diatonic chord scales. Each of the modes works over a certain type of chord because it contains the tones of that chord. Here are some examples:

CHORD TYPE	CHORD SCALE	EXPLANATION
Major Triad	Major scale	All three notes in a major chord (1, 3 and 5) are in the major scale.
Dominant 7	Mixolydian mode	All four notes in a dominant 7 chord (1, 3, 5 and $\flat$7) are in the Mixolydian mode.
Minor 7	Dorian mode	All four notes in a minor 7 chord (1, $\flat$3, 5 and $\flat$7) are in the Dorian mode.

Later you will learn that there are more possibilities, but chord scales are commonly used to play "*inside*" (diatonically). If you play the notes from a chord scale in a bass line, you will still sound "inside;" you will be using diatonic passing tones to step from chord tone to chord tone.

Example 23 is a bass line using just the chord tones of the dominant 7 chord (1, 3, 5, $\flat$7). It traces the chord with arpeggios, moving in skips rather than steps.

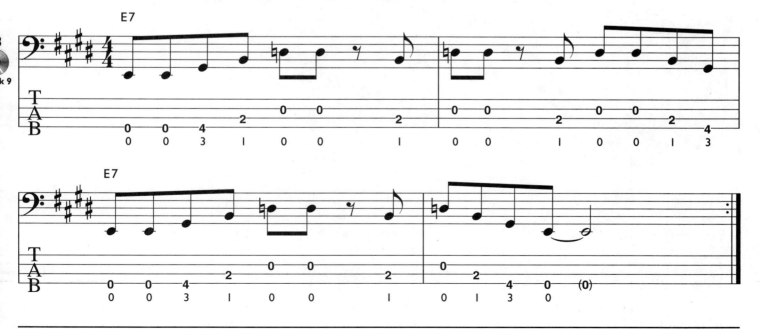

Example 24 is a bass line using notes of the dominant 7 chord scale, the Mixolydian mode. Notice how the passing tones allow for a smoother bass line than the bass line on the bottom of page 17.

John Pattitucci is a virtuoso bass player who is equally adept at upright bass and electric bass. He has played with many of today's top jazz musicians including pianist Chick Corea (check out the Elektric Band CD, released in 1990).

CHROMATIC PASSING TONES

Chromatic passing tones are non-diatonic tones that connect scale tones, and as the name implies, they move chromatically (in half steps). These tones are usually found in music such as jazz where chromaticism is common, but are also used in other styles to "spice up" the bass line. Walking bass lines with chromatic passing tones sound very hip.

Here is an example of a bass line using chromatic passing tones which are circled in the music.

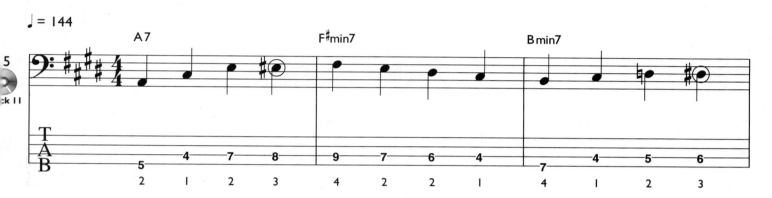

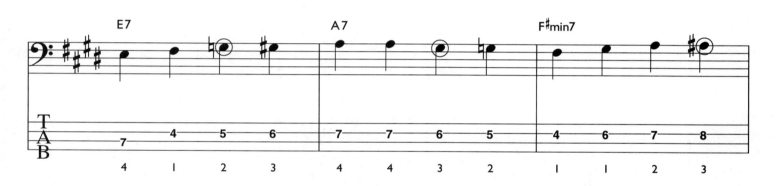

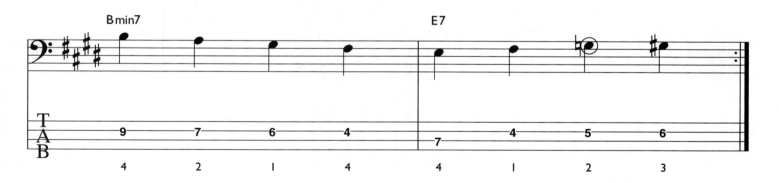

Approach notes are often found in jazz walking bass lines. They can be a whole step above, a whole step below, a half step above or a half step below the targeted chord tone and are approached by *leap* (an interval larger than a 2nd). You won't find them in a heavy metal bass line that consists of sixteenth note rhythms on the root of the chord. Approach notes help make chord changes flow by giving smooth movement from one chord to the next.

The examples below show the tones of a C7 chord with approach notes. Chord tones are circled.

* = Approach note

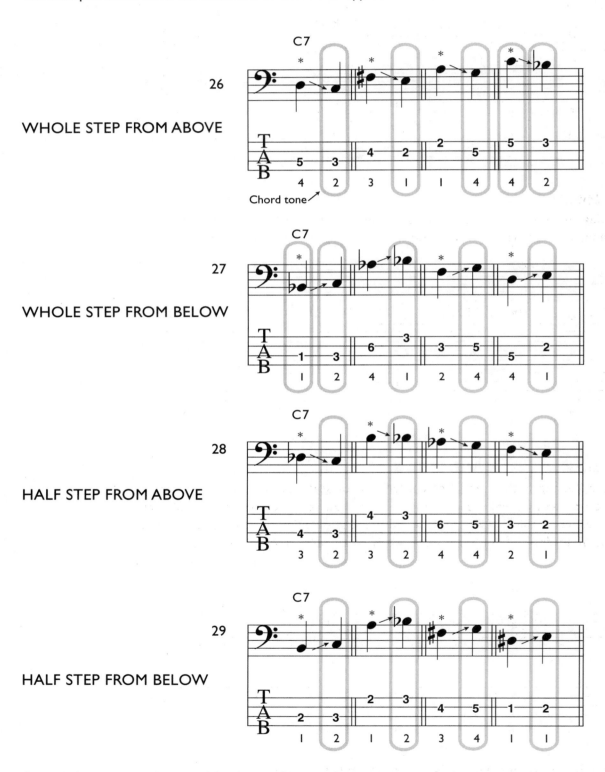

WHOLE STEP FROM ABOVE

WHOLE STEP FROM BELOW

HALF STEP FROM ABOVE

HALF STEP FROM BELOW

Approach notes are discussed further in Chapter 2.

The term *minor scale* refers to a seven-note scale with a minor 3rd (♭3) above the tonic. There are three forms of the minor scale. They are shown below.

NATURAL MINOR

If you play a major scale starting and ending on the 6th degree, you have a natural minor scale. Compared to a major scale with the same root, the natural minor scale has a ♭3, ♭6 and ♭7.

HARMONIC MINOR

Raise the 7th degree of a natural minor scale (♮7) and you have a harmonic minor scale. Compared to a major scale with the same root, the harmonic minor scale has a ♭3 and a ♭6.

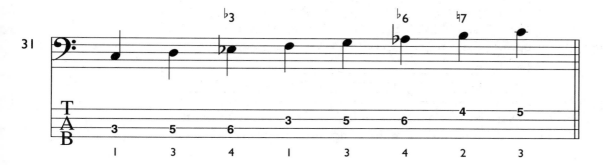

MELODIC MINOR

Raise the 6th and 7th degrees (♮6 and ♮7) of a natural minor scale, and you have the melodic minor scale. Compared to a major scale with the same root, the melodic minor scale has a ♭3. Classical musicians think of the scale as descending differently than it ascends, but other musicians often don't. For that reason, this is often called the *jazz minor* scale.

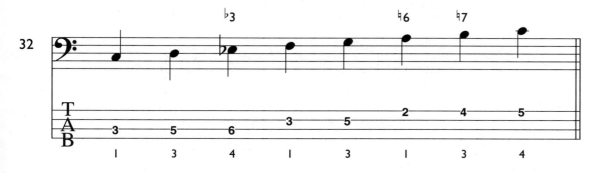

Chord progressions based on minor scales are discussed in Chapter 3.

CHAPTER 2

Rhythm Changes

A common song form in jazz (second only to the blues) is the chord progression—the *changes*—from *I've Got Rhythm*, a tune composed by George Gershwin in the 1930s. The changes, known as *Rhythm Changes*, are fun to play over. The basic chord progression is the I-vi-IV-V progression you learned in *Beginning Electric Bass*. There is a *bridge* (a transition from one theme to another) of four dominant 7 chords lasting two bars each, going around the circle of 5ths (see page 6).

In a jazz context, musicians commonly use many chord *substitutions,* and "*blowing*" (soloing) over the changes can get pretty wild. Substitutions are chords that are used in place of the regular chords of a progression. Because of certain similarities to the regular chords, they fill the functions of those chords in the progression, but add color and interest. You experienced lots of substitutions already on page 72 of *Intermediate Electric Bass* when we looked at all the different ways of varying the twelve-bar blues in B$\flat$.

But like the blues, the Rhythm Changes can be found in thousands of tunes outside of jazz. If you turn on the radio, you will hear quite a few tunes that use the first four chords of Rhythm Changes as the harmonic structure for the tune; from old rhythm and blues tunes like *Stand By Me* by Ben E. King and Lieber and Stoller, to tunes like *Every Breath You Take* by The Police. The foundation for both of these tunes is the I-vi-IV-V chord progression, the first four bars of Rhythm Changes.

Pop and rock tunes usually don't use the *bridge* (the transition section) of Rhythm Changes. The bridge is great for blowing over, but pop and rock music is not composed with the intention of improvising throughout the tune, therefore the bridge usually doesn't follow the circle of 5ths.

The point here is that practicing, memorizing and learning the sound of Rhythm Changes will help you put another few hundred tunes under your belt. This chapter will discuss improvising bass lines on Rhythm Changes. The jazz context offers more freedom in the bass line, but you can use the material in this chapter in many of your playing situations.

After working through this chapter, turn on the radio and try to pick out some tunes using this chord progression!

Below is the original set of changes for Rhythm Changes. It will be used to explore some bass line possibilities.

Let's concentrate on the first eight bars of the Rhythm Changes progression. There are two chords per measure, with two beats per chord. That is not much time! Here are the steps for developing a bass line over quick-moving changes:

PLAY THE ROOTS
The first step is to get comfortable with the root motion by just playing the root.

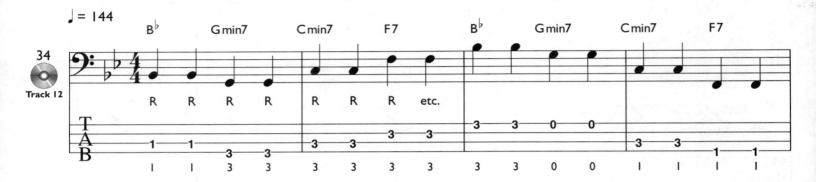

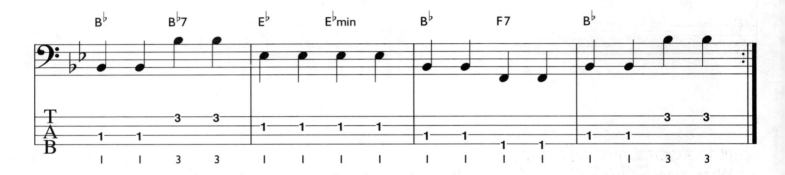

PLAY ROOTS AND 5THS
Adding the 5th of the chord will help the bass line move. Notice that the 5th can be played in any octave, below or above the root.

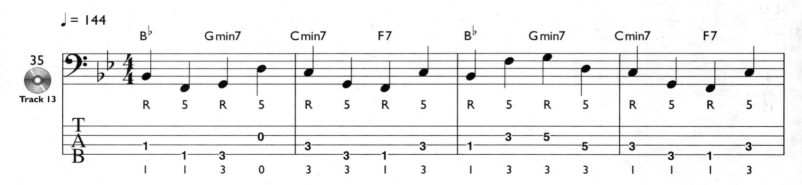

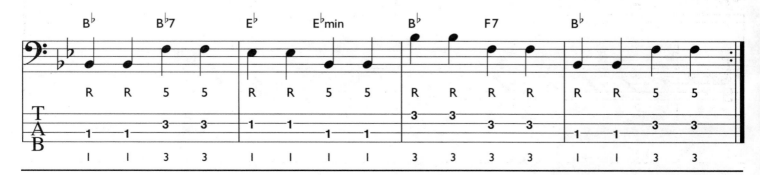

ADD THE 3RD

The 3rd of the chord will add "color" to the bass line. The 3rd determines whether the chord is major or minor. Because just roots and 3rds are used, the bass line will not move very smoothly.

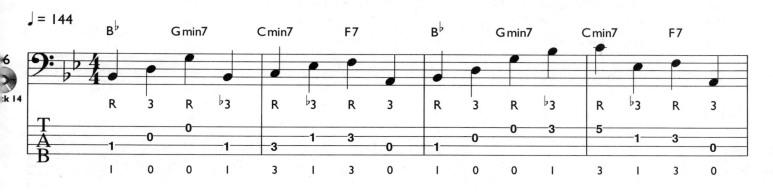

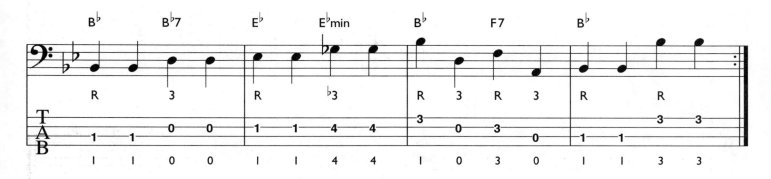

PLAY ROOTS, 3RDS AND 5THS

When you are comfortable with the roots, 3rds and 5ths, you can combine them to make the bass line flow very easily and sound great.

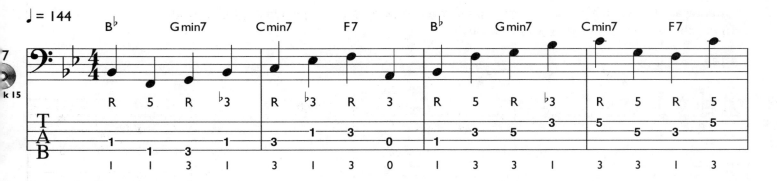

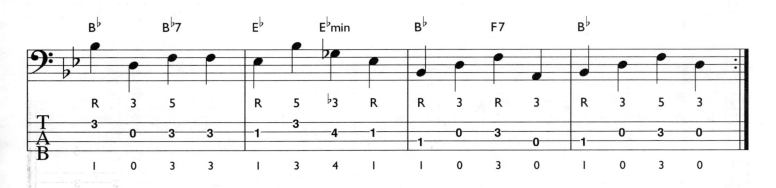

ADD APPROACH NOTES

Passing tones and approach notes were reviewed in Chapter 1 of this book. There is a more detailed discussion in Chapter 7 of *Intermediate Electric Bass*.

So far, you have played bass lines on Rhythm Changes using the root, 3rd and 5th tones of the chords. Now, to help the walking bass line sound more "jazzy," we will precede the first note of each new chord with an approach note a half step above.

Check it out. It sounds great!

* = Approach note

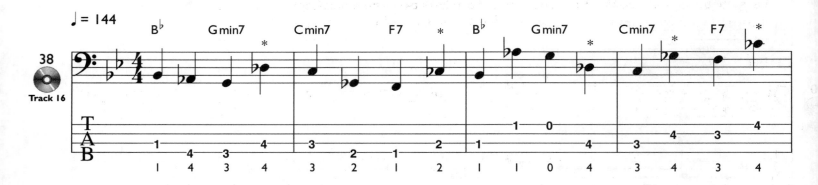

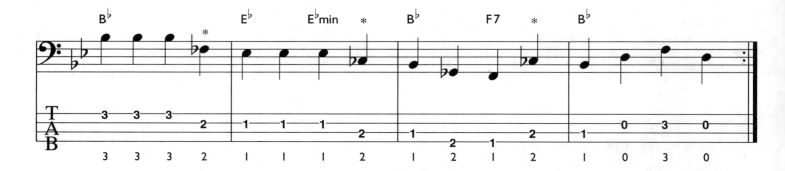

Below are the same eight bars of Rhythm Changes. In this example, the first note of each new chord is approached by a half step below.

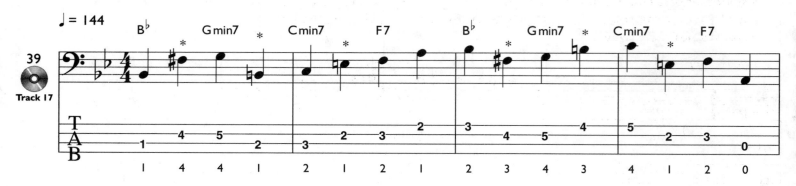

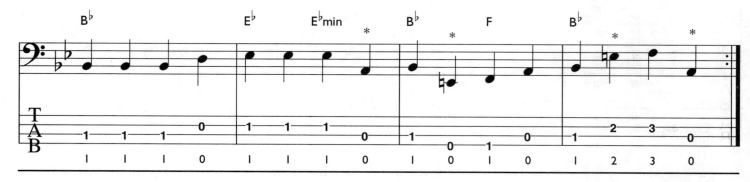

The Rhythm Changes progression has four sections. Three of them have the I-vi-IV-V progression. This is the "A" section. The bridge is the "B" section. The overall form is A-A-B-A. Unlike the "A" section, each chord in the bridge lasts for two bars, or eight beats. This gives you more time to explore each chord and use a walking bass line (see Chapter 7, *Intermediate Electric Bass*). Here are the steps for developing a bass line over the bridge:

USE JUST CHORD TONES

Let's start using just chord tones. Since each chord lasts two whole measures, we need to incorporate more notes than the root and 5th so the line will be a walking line.

ADD PASSING TONES

This line will use passing tones, both diatonic and chromatic. The passing tones allow for a smoother bass line. Notice that measures 3 and 7 of this bass line start on the 5th of the chord and not the root. This is always an available choice, but not the only one. The passing tones are circled.

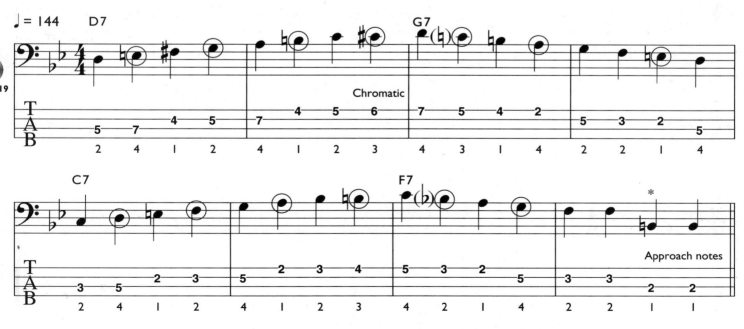

Now it is time to play through the whole form (AABA) of Rhythm Changes. The following bass line combines all of the ideas discussed in this chapter. Take the time to analyze the bass line so that you know where every note came from and how it functions. Analyzing any written bass lines you can get your hands on, or even those you have learned from recordings, will help your understanding of the construction of bass lines. Look for diatonic passing tones, chromatic passing tones, arpeggios, approach notes, etc. Mark them in pencil. You will learn a lot!

RHYTHM CHANGES LINE #1

Track 20

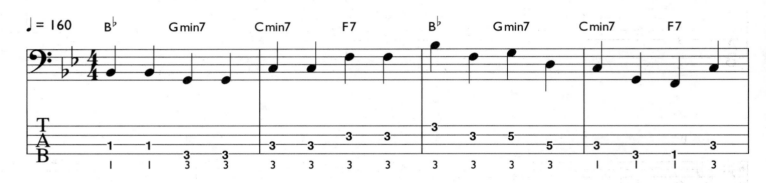

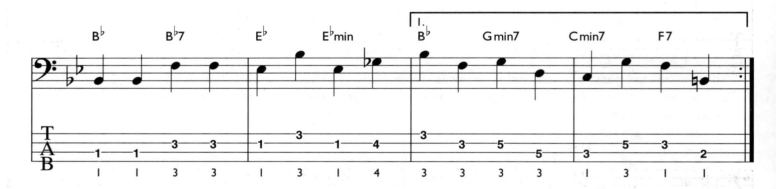

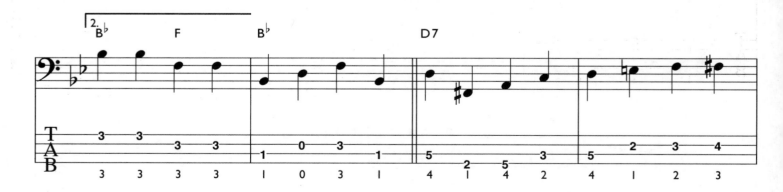

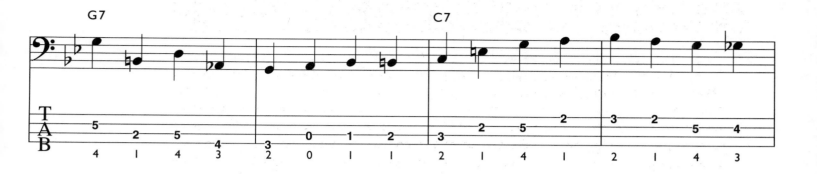

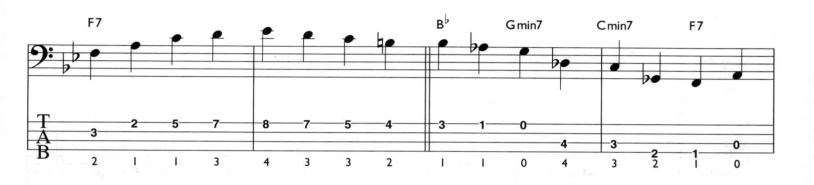

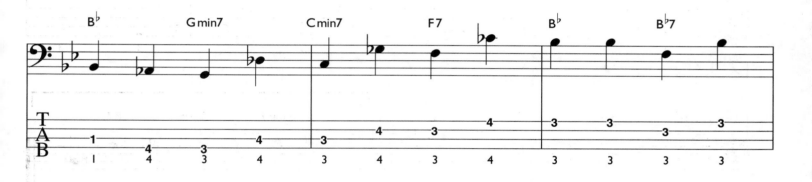

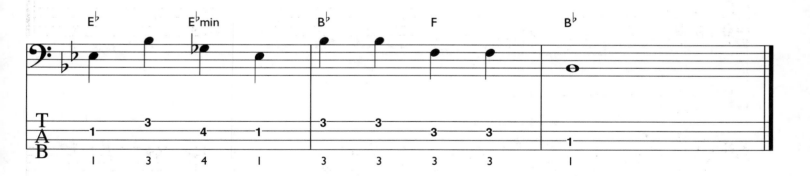

Here is a variation of the Rhythm Changes chord progression that emerged in the 1930s.
Notice the following three variations:

1) The use of diminished chords
2) The Gmin7 chord has been changed to G7
3) The Dmin7 chord sometimes substitutes for the B♭ chord

RHYTHM CHANGES LINE #2

Track 21

Here is a list of just a few of the many tunes that are based on Rhythm Changes:

PIECE	COMPOSER
Anthropology	Charlie Parker
Moose the Mooch	Charlie Parker
Oleo	Sonny Rollins
Rhythm-A-Ning	Thelonious Monk
The Serpent's Tooth	Miles Davis
The Theme	Miles Davis

The 3rd and 7th chord tones of a dominant chord form an interval of a diminished 5th (or augmented 4th—same thing). We also call this interval a *tritone*, because it is a distance of three whole steps ("tri" is the Greek word for "three"). You also know the interval as a $\flat$5 (or $\sharp$4). The dissonant tritone interval is what makes the dominant 7 sound unstable—as if it wants to resolve to someplace, often to the I chord. Even if you play just the 3rd and the 7th of the dominant 7 chord, though it may sound incomplete, it still sounds like a V chord. What is unusual about the tritone in any dominant 7 chord is that it's the 3rd and 7th of not just one, but *two* dominant 7 chords.

For example, in a C7 chord (C-E-G-B$\flat$), the tritone is between the E (3) and B$\flat$ ($\flat$7). If we enharmonically respell the E to be F$\flat$, we can think it as the $\flat$7 of a G$\flat$7 chord (G$\flat$-B$\flat$-D$\flat$-F$\flat$). The B$\flat$ is the 3rd. So, the same tritone is present in the C7 and G$\flat$7 chords!

G$\flat$7 can substitute for C7. And dig this: G$\flat$ is a tritone above C! We have two good reasons for calling this a *tritone substitution: the tritones in a dominant 7 chord and another dominant 7 chord a tritone higher are the same.*

Tritone substitution is often used to create chromatic bass lines.

Emin7	A7	Dmin7	G7	CMaj7
	$\downarrow$ tritone		$\downarrow$ tritone	
Emin7	E$\flat$7	Dmin7	D$\flat$7	CMaj7

You can also precede a tritone substitution (or any dominant 7 chord) with the ii chord.

ii	V	I	Explanation
Dmin7	G7	CMaj7	ii-V-I in C
Dmin7	D$\flat$7	CMaj7	The same ii-V-I, but with the tritone substitution in place of G7.
Dmin7	A$\flat$min7-D$\flat$7	CMaj7	The tritone substitution (D$\flat$7) preceded by its ii chord (A$\flat$min7).
A$\flat$min7	D$\flat$7	CMaj7	The tritone substitution and its ii chord replacing Dmin7-G7.

There are lots of more complex substitution possibilities. There are plenty of theory books that teach about this, such as *Theory for the Contemporary Guitarist*, by Guy Capuzzo.

Let's take a look and see how tritone substitution is used in Rhythm Changes.

In Rhythm Changes, it is common for tritone substitution chords to be used on the bridge of the tune. Below are two examples of the bridge of Rhythm Changes. The first example shows the original set of changes, the second example uses tritone substitution.

Original Changes	D7	D7	G7	G7	C7	C7	F7	F7
			$\downarrow$	$\downarrow$			$\downarrow$	$\downarrow$
With Tritone Substitutions	D7	D7	D$\flat$7	D$\flat$7	C7	C7	C$\flat$7	C$\flat$7

This last variation of Rhythm Changes uses tritone substitutions in a few places. Compare this progression to the one on page 30 and see if you can find where the tritone substitutions occur*. Writing out bass lines on all of the versions of Rhythm Changes discussed in this chapter will be a good exercise in thinking about the chords and will teach you a lot. Once you write them, they are always there to play.

* ANSWERS: Measure 3, third beat. Measure 4, third beat. Measure 7, third beat. Measure 13. measure 17. Measure 21, third beat. Measure 22, third beat.

CHAPTER 3

Minor Blues

In *Beginning Electric Bass*, you learned about the diatonic harmony of a major scale and learned about major-key chord progressions. In order to learn about the minor blues, you need to learn about diatonic harmony in minor keys.

MINOR DIATONIC HARMONY

Remember, there are three forms of the minor scale: natural minor, harmonic minor and melodic minor (see page 21). Each one has its own diatonic harmony. Here are the three forms of the minor scale in C, harmonized with 7 chords:

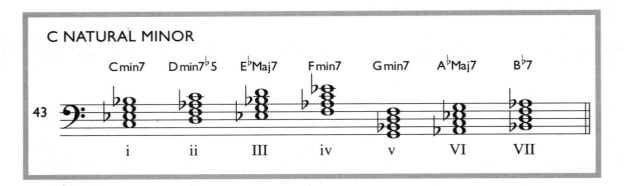

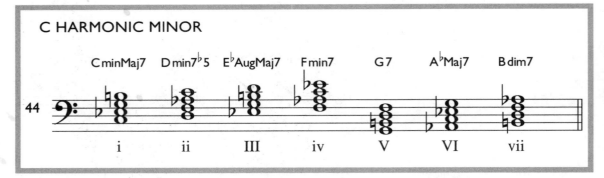

minMaj7 = 1 ♭3 5 7
AugMaj7 = 1 3 ♯5 7

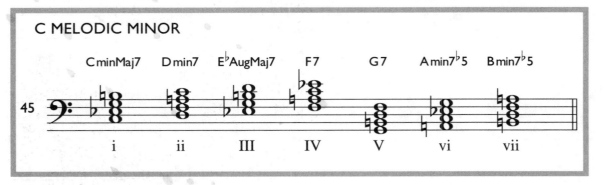

Like the major blues, the minor blues is based on the i, iv and V chords of the key (remember, minor chords are indicated with lower case Roman numerals). The V chord of the natural minor scale is not dominant (see page 34) but in a minor blues, the V7 chord is often borrowed from the harmonic minor scale, which has a dominant chord on the 5th scale degree. Notice that the turnaround (last four bars) uses different chords than those in a major blues. The chords used are ♭VI7-V7-i. The ♭VI7 is one half step lower than the VI.

Here is a C Minor blues:

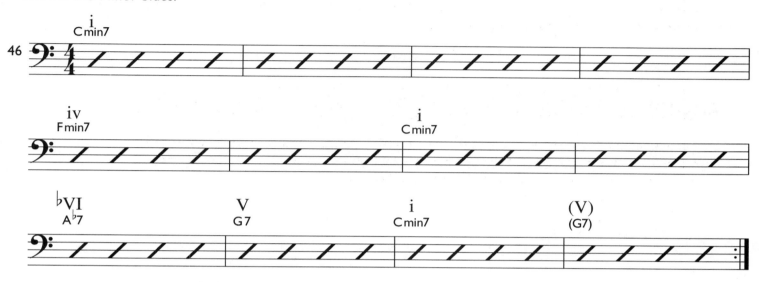

Roscoe Beck is best known for his bass work with Eric Johnson and Robben Ford. He co-founded the band The Blue Line with guitarist Robben Ford. Since the 1980s, he has produced records for other artists such as Jennifer Warnes.

The minor blues song form has been used to create many blues and jazz tunes. Here is a rhythm & blues bass line on a minor blues. This bass line is in the style of the one played on B.B. King's *The Thrill Is Gone*.

This minor blues bass line is in the style of Roscoe Beck, bassist with blues guitar wizard, Robben Ford.

Here are a couple of walking bass lines on a minor blues.

Example 50 includes some *altered dominant* chords. Altered dominant chords are dominant 7 chords with added extensions, such as the 9th, that have been altered. A 9th is
simply a note nine scale degrees above the root of the chord. For example, the 9th of an
E7 chord is F♯, because if you build a major scale on E, and go one more note past the
octave (8), you get F♯, which is just an octave above the 2nd. Now, if you alter F♯ by raising
it a half step (G), you have a ♯9.

CHAPTER 4

Latin Grooves

The term "Latin music" is tossed around very loosely. It refers to music from South America, especially Brazil. Musicians such as Pat Metheny and many others have been influenced by and recorded with Brazilian musicians. Check out all of the Brazilian music that you can! Much of this chapter will be concerned with *salsa* music, which is a popular style that combines rock and Latin elements.

THE CLAVE

The most unique and important aspect of Afro-Cuban music is the rhythmic pattern known as the *clave* (pronounced "clah-vay"). It ia also the name of a percussion instrument made of two wood sticks. The clave rhythm is often referred to as *rumba clave* and it is a two-bar rhythmic pattern. The clave occurs in two forms, the 3:2 clave (*forward clave*), and the 2:3 clave (*reverse clave*). Notice that the rhythms are written in cut time ¢ (♩ = one beat). Pay special attention to the dots and ties as you practice counting and clapping these rhythms.

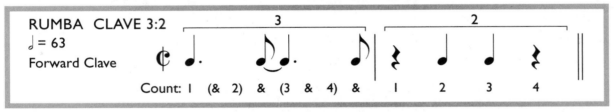

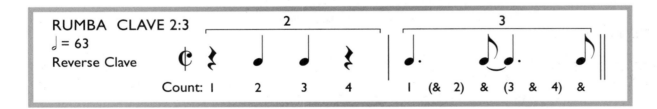

The *son clave* (also 3:2 or 2:3), doesn't displace the last eighth note.

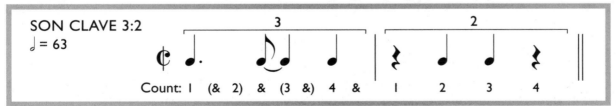

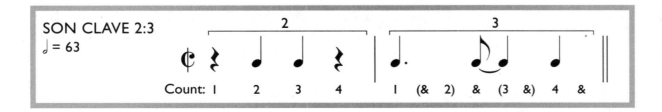

THE TUMBAO

In salsa music, the bass *tumbao* is the heart of the tune. A tumbao is a repeated figure that creates the groove.

A great exercise to internalize the clave is to practice tapping it with your foot while playing a tumbao. Many great players use this method. It is very challenging, so don't be discouraged if you can't do it right away.

BOSSA NOVA

It is not in the scope of this book to discuss the history of these rhythms. But it is important to at least know the names and sounds and be able to play them. *Bossa Nova* is a dance rhythm with a dotted quarter/eighth note feel. After playing these bass lines take a trip to the good ol' library and study the origins of these rhythms. Then go to a record store, buy some recordings of Brazilian music and get the rhythms in your ears!

 BOSSA NOVA GROOVE #1

Track 26

Check out this next tune! The bass part is a bossa nova groove. The melody is included so you can play the tune with a friend. Otherwise, if you have the CD available with this book, you can play along with some great players.

BOSSA NOVA GROOVE #2

Track 27

THE MAMBO, THE GUAJIRA AND THE CHA-CHA

Throughout the 1930s, '40s, and '50s, many jazz and Latin bandleaders integrated African rhythmic structures with European harmonies. In Cuba and Puerto Rico, the results of this combination led to a variety of musical styles and dances. The *mambo*, *guajira* and the *cha-cha* are just a few of the many.

MAMBO
Here is a mambo. The pulse is felt in cut-time.

This is a variation.

Gary Willis was a member of Tribal Tech, an important jazz-fusion ensemble he co-lead with guitarist Scott Henderson. In September, 1996, Willis launched his solo career with the release of "No Sweat."

Here is a three-chord mambo example.

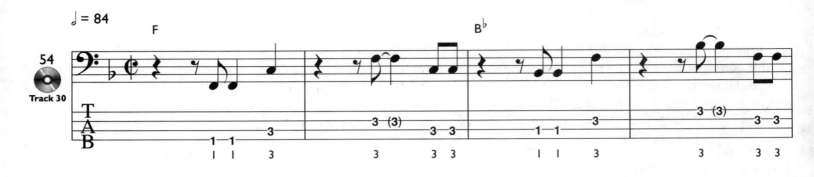

Here is another variation. This one moves between three chords.

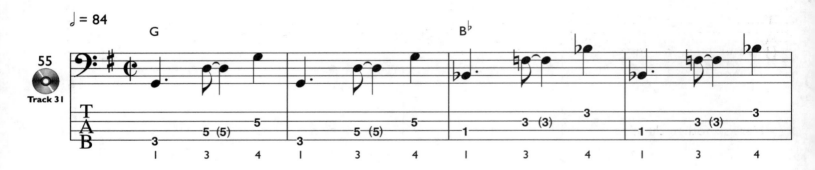

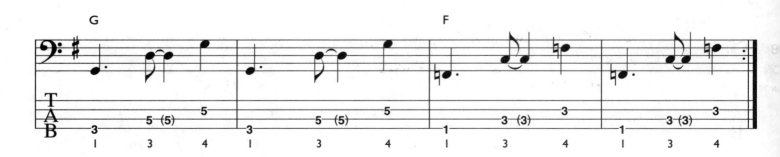

GUAJIRA

The pulse is in four. The stresses are felt on the "&" after "1," and the downbeats of "3" and "4."

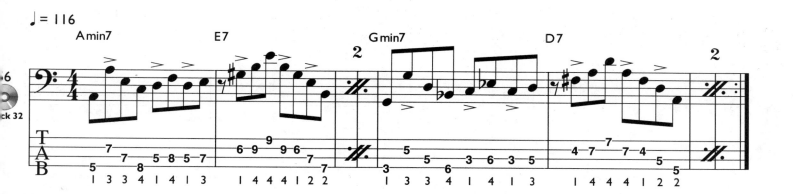

CHA-CHA

The cha-cha groove is usually played at a medium tempo, around ♩ = 80 to 140.

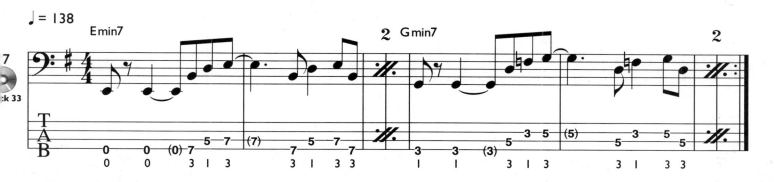

Here's another cha-cha:

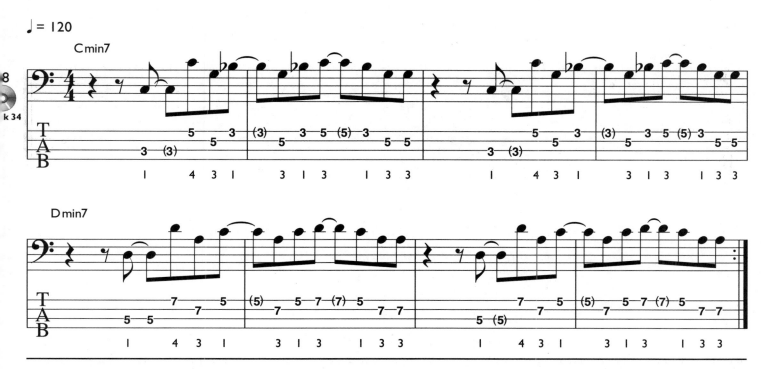

Latin music can make its own brand of funk. Here are a couple of funky grooves over the 3:2 forward clave.

Here are two funky grooves over the 2:3 reverse clave.

LATIN ROCK

The next line is in the style of a Bo Diddley groove. The groove is based on the 2:3 reverse clave. Check out some of the great Latin rock tunes on Paul Simon recordings. Several superb bassists, including Marcus Miller and Anthony Jackson, appear on Simon's records and supply some great grooves.

 ## ONE FOR BO

Track 39

Now that you've played through some Latin and Afro-Cuban bass lines, turn on the radio and listen for some Latin tunes. When you find one, try to figure out the bass line and determine which clave is being used, the 3:2 or 2:3.

Hopefully, you agree that Latin and Afro-Cuban bass lines are fun to play. The bass parts are different from what you may be used to because of the displacement of the beat and the clave.

Here is a list of recordings of some great Afro-Cuban and Latin music. This list is pretty diverse. Some of the recordings are jazzy, some are funky and some are popular songs. Get as many recordings as you can. The more you listen to this music, the more you will internalize it.

Enjoy!

ARTISTS	RECORDINGS
Ruben Blades and Seis de Solar	"Live"
Michel Camilo	"Michel Camilo"
Jerry Gonzalez & The Fort Apache Band	"Obatala"
The Meters	"Struttin'"
Eddie Palmieri	"The Sun of Latin Music"
Tito Puente	"Goza Mi Timbal"
Dave Valetine	"Live at the Blue Note"

You can learn a lot about Afro-Cuban and Latin bass playing just by listening to the following three bass players.

Sal Cuevas
Lincoln Goines
Andy Gonzalez

CHAPTER 5

Reggae

Ya, Mon! This is a fun music to play. In reggae music, the guitar player is the timekeeper. Although there are variations, the guitar commonly plays chords on beats 2 and 4. The bass and/or drums fill in beats 1 and 3. The bass player usually lays down a repetitive line that locks in with both the guitar and drum parts. When a reggae band is clicking, the groove can be hypnotic. Reggae bass lines usually use a warm, fat tone by adjusting the tone controls on the amplifier for a lot of bass and not much treble. The parts are played mostly in the lower range of the bass.

Everybody has heard of Bob Marley! Listening to his music will give you the feel for this style of music. Reggae crept into popular music when Sting and The Police incorporated reggae grooves and bass lines into their tunes. Many others, including Elvis Costello, Blondie and NOFX have experimented with the style, too.

Below is a guitar rhythm that is commonly found in reggae grooves. There is a sample bass line included so that you can hear the interaction between the two instruments. Often, the guitar player will use upstrokes to play these chords. Guitarists call this kind of playing *skanking*. If don't have the CD available for this book, have a friend play the chords using this rhythm while you play the bass lines on the following pages.

V = Upstroke on the guitar.

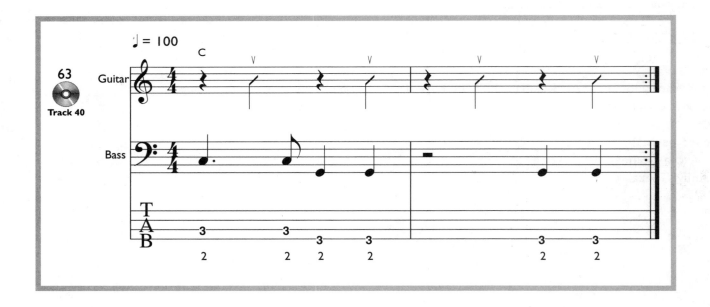

Reggae bass lines are usually chordal bass lines. This means that the line consists of mostly chord tones. Scale tones are sometimes used for a smooth line, but there is very little chromaticism in this music. Remember, whenever you are playing reggae bass lines, lay back, relax, play in the pocket and have fun, *Rasta Mon!*

The following pages of this chapter are filled with reggae bass lines. Although these lines are written in $\frac{4}{4}$, since the drum part often emphasizes beat 3, they feel like there are two beats per measure.

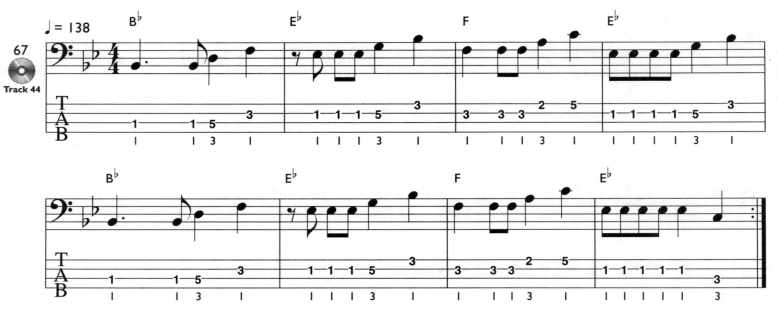

The next two examples include quarter-note triplets. Play three quarter notes in the time of two. Here's a way to count it using two eighth-note triplets (play on the underlined counts): _**1**_ trip-_**let**_, 2 _**trip**_-let. Just count two eighth-note triplets and play on every other count. Also, it is helpful to start thinking in eighth-note triplets in the last beat of the previous bar.

Notice the use of dead notes. They add a great effect to the bass line.

Play this line very slowly at first. Give special attention to the dotted eighth/sixteenth note rhythm.

Here is a reggae tune for you to play through. The melody is included so that you can play the tune with a friend. If your friend is not available, it is best you gete the CD that is available with this book, so that you can play along.

RASTA RON

Track 56

♩ = 138

Here are a few reggae artists that you should check out:

> Jimmy Cliff
> Bob Marley
> Steel Pulse

You might think about taking your next vacation in Jamaica to soak up some sun and get this music in your soul.

Sting started out as the bassist and the principal singer in the British super-group, The Police. Their style was highly influenced by Jamaican reggae music. When The Police disbanded at the peak of their career in 1983, Sting went on to release a number of highly acclaimed solo albums.

CHAPTER 6

Ska

Some will argue that there are different periods of ska music and that it is different than reggae in many ways. Others will argue that it is basically reggae with a *double-time* (twice as fast) feel. The drum groove is like reggae in cut time. The bass parts are not drastically different, except they are a little less busy because of the faster tempos. The guitar part, like in reggae music, often plays on beats 2 ands 4.

Many ska tunes of today are blended with rhythms from many other styles of music. The music of groups like the Mighty, Mighty Bosstones are good examples of some great contemporary ska music.

Here is a sample rhythm guitar part and bass line:

Have fun with these contemporary ska bass lines. Watch out, the tempos are pretty fast!

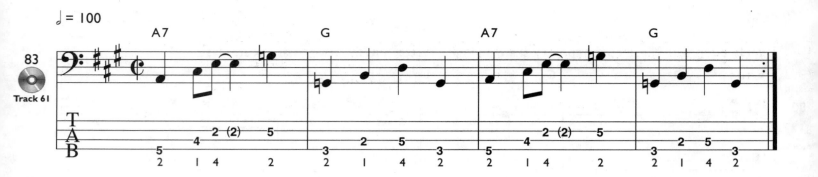

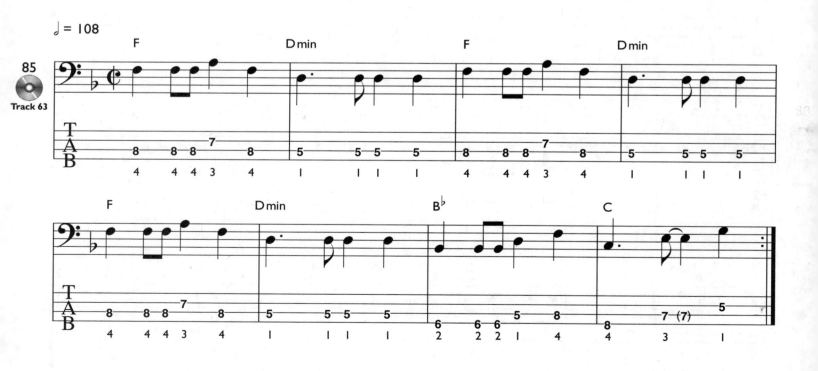

Here is a ska tune for you to play through. The melody is included so that you can play this with some friends and work on your ska "chops." You can also play along with the CD that is available for this book if you have it. Notice the G/B chord in measure 8. This is a *slash* chord. The symbol on the left is the name of the chord. The bass note is indicated to the right of the slash.

SKA FOR MA'

Track 67

Some ska bands you might want to check out are:

> Mighty, Mighty Bosstones
> The Pietasters
> Toasters

CHAPTER 7

Advanced Funk Bass Lines

Funk bass lines were discussed in both *Beginning Electric Bass* and *Intermediate Electric Bass*. Although the funk lines in this book are more difficult, the funk and slap & pop chapters in the other books also offer the advanced player some challenging and funky bass lines. The funk lines in this chapter utilize the diatonic and chromatic passing tones that are discussed in detail towards the end of *Intermediate Electric Bass*. Using passing tones will make your funk bass lines sound jazzier. Although you can create very funky bass lines without using them, great players produce killer funk lines when using all of their weapons, including passing tones. The late Jaco Pastorius, one of the greatest funk bassists of all time, used lots of passing tones in his lines.

PIZZICATO FUNK
The term *pizzicato* refers to the plucking of the string as most bassists do, with the fingers of the right hand. Jaco Pastorius played some of the funkiest bass lines ever, and never used the slap & pop technique. He had an impeccable sixteenth-note feel and, coupled with his note choices and great technique, was a master of pizzicato funk. Pastorius, who lived in Florida when he hit the scene in 1976, often incorporated Afro-Cuban and Latin rhythms in his funk playing. Tragically, he died at 35, but he had left his mark on the bass world long before then.

Another excellent funk player that doesn't use the slap & pop technique is Rocco Prestia of the group Tower of Power. Prestia just lays back, never solos and is very unassuming, but plays some very hip pizzicato funk bass lines. You may have heard the Tower of Power anthem *What Is Hip*.

The predecessor to both Pastorius and Prestia was James Jamerson. He was solely responsible for the Motown bass sound. His bass parts were as significant as the vocal line. Whomever Jamerson was recording for would ask him to come up with his own part, knowing it would smoke whatever written part was there. All bassists should check out what he did. It was innovative, and he was the first master of pizzicato funk.

SLAP & POP FUNK
Around the time when Pastorius hit the scene, so did another great player who was also responsible for influencing a generation of bass players. That was Stanley Clarke. Clarke certainly wasn't the first bassist to use the slap technique, but while most bass players were playing slap grooves on a single chord (one-chord funk), he would slap over chord progressions. A host of players, such as Marcus Miller, Darryl Jones, Mark King, Bootsy Collins and others, helped popularize the slap & pop technique.

Since Pastorius and Clarke in the 1970s, a lot of great players have come along and blessed us with some great playing. But the greatest innovator for the electric bass since Pastorius is, without a doubt, the one and only Victor Wooten, whose combination of inventiveness, technique and musicianship has made him one greatest electric players ever.

The following pages of this chapter are filled with funk bass lines. The first half will be pizzicato funk grooves. The second half will be slap & pop funk grooves.

Here are two symbols you should be aware of, since you will see them used in the grooves in this chapter.

X = Dead note

H = Hammer-on

PIZZICATO FUNK GROOVES

Play these grooves slowly at first. After you have played each groove correctly, play along with the CD available for this book if you have it. Then try to play these grooves with your friends.

♩ = 104

Jaco Pastorius was born in Fort Lauderdale on December 1st, 1951, the son of a jazz drummer. He went on to define a new style of electric bass playing that not only revolutionized the jazz bass, but redefined the disciplines of fusion, rock and R&B. In the 1970s, he played with the fusion group Weather Report, founded by pianist Joe Zawinul and saxophonist Wayne Shorter. In the 1980s, he toured with his big band, Word of Mouth. He died tragically in 1987 at the age of 35.

Be careful with these grooves. There are lots of dead notes and they are a little tricky to play. The grooves on this page are in the style of Jaco Pastorius. Notice the use of *slides*. Just glide your finger along the string to the destination fret. Do not pluck the second note in the slide. Good Luck!

SL = Slide

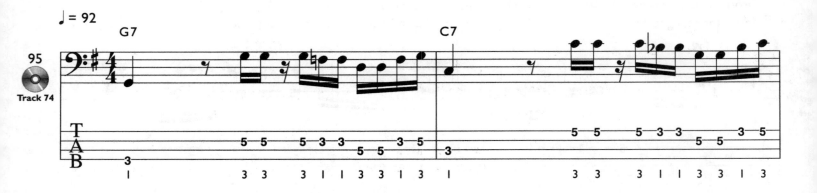

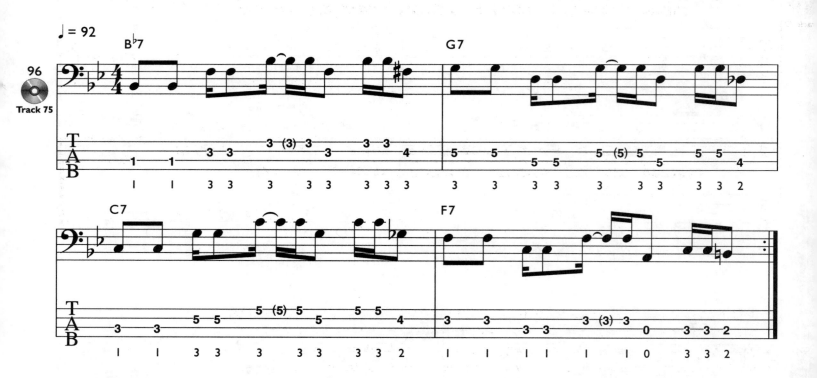

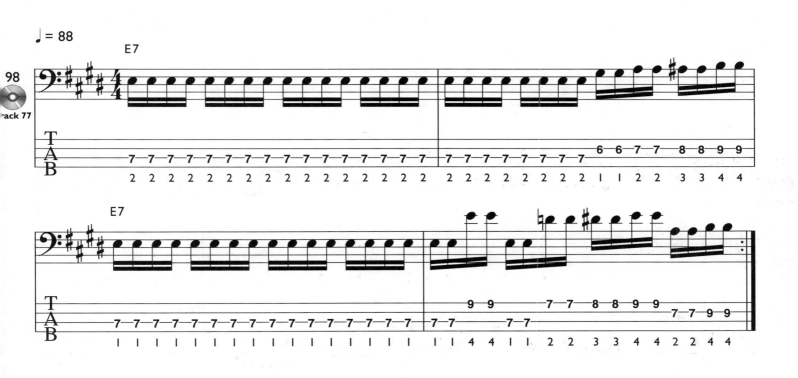

When playing bass lines with a lot of notes, it is important that you do it in the context of the tune. Don't take away from the music. Add to it. Listen to Pastorius' and Prestia's bass lines. Even though there might be a lot going on in the music, their bass lines are very musical, almost percussive, and are never forced for the sake of the bass part. They don't detract from the music.

For a review of slap & pop symbols, refer to the Key on page 16.

In examples 99 to 103, the S symbol for slap technique is not used. Assume all notes are slapped unless there is a mark for a pop, hammer-on, dead note or pull-off. Any technique other than a slap is marked with the appropriate symbol. Every note without a symbol should be played with the thumb, using the slap technique. There are no normally plucked notes.

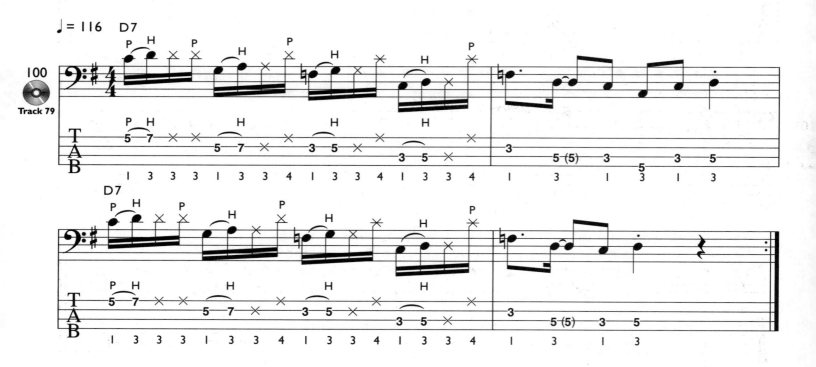

THE DOUBLE POP

The *double pop* is a technique used by many bassists including Victor Wooten and Marcus Miller. It refers to popping two notes in succession. Use the right-hand 1st finger ⊓ for the first pop and the 2nd finger ∨ for the second pop. This is a tricky technique and requires a lot of practice, so try these lines slowly at first.

THE DOUBLE-STOP

A *double stop* is when you play two notes at once. This is done using the 1st and 2nd fingers of the right hand. Place them on adjacent strings simultaneously and pull both across the strings together. Obviously, this can't be done with the normal rest-stroke technique described in beginning of *Beginning Electric Bass*. Rather, it is done with a *free-stroke*, where the fingers move through the strings and up into the palm instead of the next string. This way, neither finger interferes with the vibration of an adjacent string. Intervals of a 3rd, 4th and 5th are commonly played as double stops.

Here are some bass lines that use double pops and double stops:

These techniques help you play some fresh sounding bass lines, but remember that the groove is the most important thing. Don't play these techniques to show off. If you overdo it you'll be taking away from the music.

Victor Wooten is a virtuoso bassist who plays with considerable technical ability in A variety of styles that appear completely effortless. His work in the 1980s and 1990s with Bela Fleck and the Flecktones, and his dazzling solo recordings, make him one of the world's top bassists.

CHAPTER 8

Rock Bass Lines in Odd Time Signatures

Most of the music that we are used to hearing is written in common time. $\frac{4}{4}$ time is the most commonly used time signature in most types of music (hence the term "common time"). Just about all of the bass lines in all three books of this method are written in $\frac{4}{4}$ time. Although $\frac{4}{4}$ time is the most widely used time signature, many bands use odd time signatures to provide some interesting grooves. Yes, Rush and Phish are just a few of the groups that explore time signatures other than $\frac{4}{4}$. Odd time signatures are used more often in jazz than in rock.

This chapter will get you started with odd time signatures. As a point of departure, here is a quick review of some basic time signatures.

 Four beats per measure
Quarter note receives one beat

The stresses are on beats 1 and 3.

 Three beats per measure
Quarter note receives one beat

The stress is on beat 1.

 Three beats per measure
Half note receives one beat

The stress is on beat 1.

 Six beats per measure
Eighth note receives one beat

Usually felt as two beats per measure, with the dotted quarter note receiving one beat. Each beat is divided into three equal pulses.

 Nine beats per measure
Eighth note receives one beat

Usually felt as three beats per measure, with the dotted quarter note receiving one beat. Each beat is divided into three equal pulses.

Ordinarily, we do not count $\frac{7}{4}$ by counting from 1 to 7. Rather, we divide the measure into a group of 3 and a group of 4. There are two ways to do this:

> 4 + 3:   1-2-3-4/1-2-3
>   1-2-3-4/5-6-7
> The accented beats are 1 and 5.

Or

> 3 + 4:   1-2-3/1-2-3-4
>   1-2-3/4-5-6-7
> The accented beats are 1 and 4.

Count this one 4 + 3.

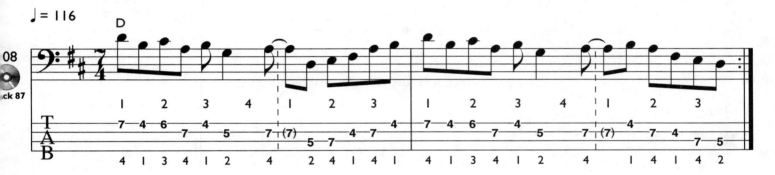

Count this one 3 + 4.

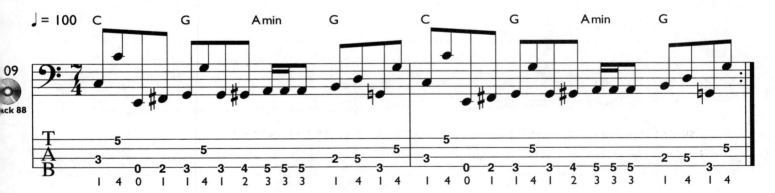

Grooves in $\frac{5}{4}$ can be counted in a straight 5. They can also be counted as 2 + 3 (1-2/1-2-3) or 3 + 2 (1-2-3/1-2).

Count this one 3 + 2.

This one is easy to count in a straight 5 since it is just straight quarter notes.

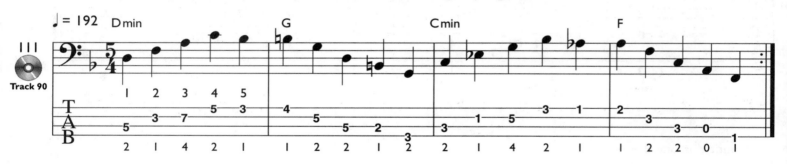

Count this one 2 + 3.

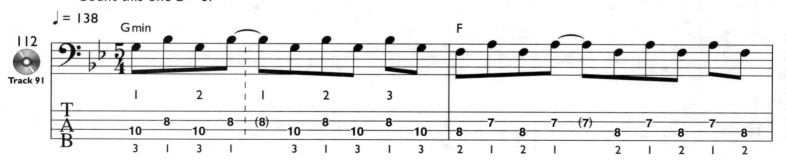

¾ is actually a very traditional time signature. We just don't use it much in rock, blues or funk music. It is sometimes called *waltz time*, after the popular 19th century dance in ¾. One cool thing about ¾ is that it has the same number of eighth notes as ⁶⁄₈ time, so the ¾ feel—with the stress on the first beat— is often alternated with the ⁶⁄₈ feel (see page 76), as in the next example.

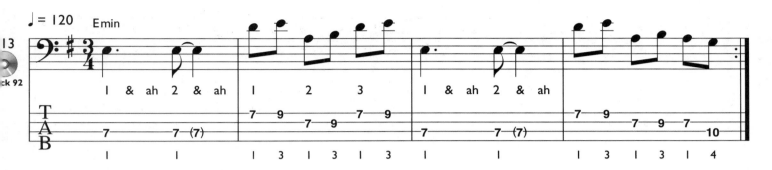

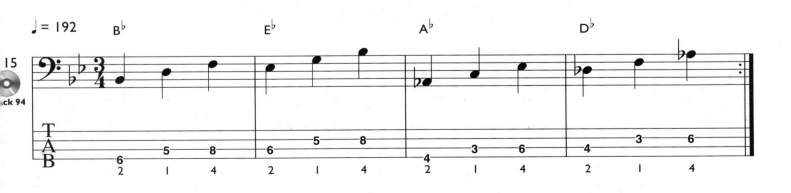

A *compound meter* is any time signature where the beat is divided into three pulses. In $\frac{4}{4}$ and $\frac{2}{4}$, the beats are divided into two eighth notes. Those are *simple meters*. In $\frac{6}{8}$ and $\frac{9}{8}$, the beats are divided into three eighth notes. The dotted quarter note equals one beat.

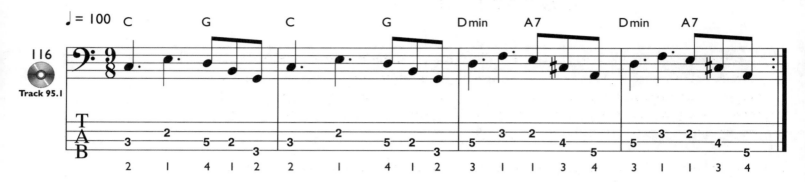

In this interesting treatment of $\frac{6}{8}$, the first three measures are subdivided into four dotted eighth notes, each of which divides into three equal sixteenths. The fourth measure is a more ordinary $\frac{6}{8}$ bar—two big beats are divided into three eighth notes each.

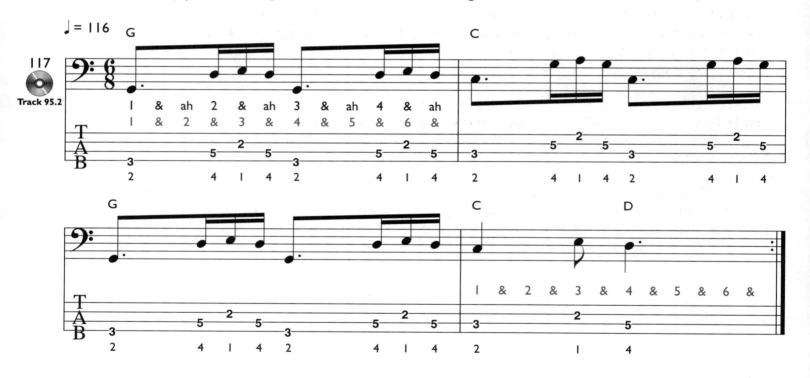

Hopefully, you had fun playing through the odd-meter bass lines in this chapter. Most music that you will play or hear will be in $\frac{4}{4}$ time. This is an area you can pursue if you have a special interest—especially if you enjoy progressive rock. If you would like to hear bassists play in odd time signatures, listen to Chris Squire of Yes, Geddy Lee of Rush, or better yet, anything by Frank Zappa!

CHAPTER 9

Improvisation

A ten-volume series of books could be filled with discussion on the topic of improvisation because there are so many approaches to teaching the subject. In a way, this three-book method has helped you learn how to improvise by providing "tools" such as chord tones, scales, passing tones, and approach notes and, hopefully, you have been successful in creating bass lines from a given set of chord changes.

This chapter will by no means be a substitute for years of practicing, listening, reading texts, taking lessons and learning from other supplementary materials. In this chapter, we will discuss a few points that will help you develop some new ideas, see things from a different perspective, or just come away with something that will help you grow as a soloist.

Throughout the history of the electric bass, the role of the instrument has evolved to the point where, in some styles of music, the bassist is expected to solo as much as any other member in the band. Everyone keeps telling you that the groove is the most important thing for the bassist, and this is true. But it is not the *only* thing that is expected from the bassist in some exciting styles of music.

Scott LaFaro, Jaco Pastorius, Stanley Clarke, Jeff Berlin, Michael Manring, John Pattitucci, Eddie Gomez and Victor Wooten are just a few of the many, many bass players that play great solos in addition to being some of the baddest groove masters of the bass world. They have the whole package.

Simply mastering the material in this chapter will not make you a great improviser. But pick out certain things that you would like to try to incorporate into your playing and practice, practice, practice and listen, listen, listen. Then, get out there and solo.

So far you have been using the 1, 3, 5 and 7 chord tones to create bass lines over chord progressions. Using these tones in arpeggios is a starting point for playing solos. Adding *extensions* to the chords will help you take this idea further. Chord extensions are scale tones 2, 4 and 6, but raised an octave to become 9, 11 and 13. Each one of these tones is simply an additional 3rd stacked above a chord; the 9 is a 3rd above the 7, the 11 is a 3rd above a 9, and a 13 is a 3rd above the 11. These extensions can be added to chord arpeggios to create a richer sound.

Here is a G Major scale with the chord extensions marked.

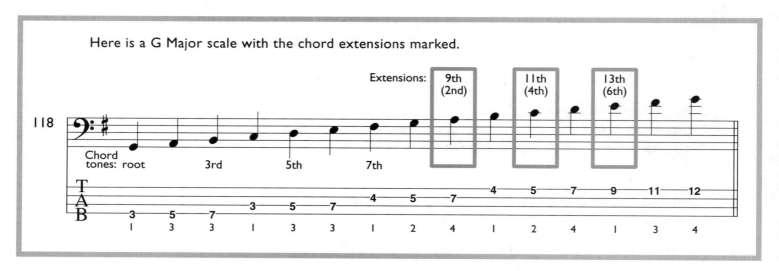

As you know, stacking 3rds creates triads and 7th chords. Here is a G Major chord with 3rds stacked above the 7. This gives you the upper diatonic extensions of the chord.

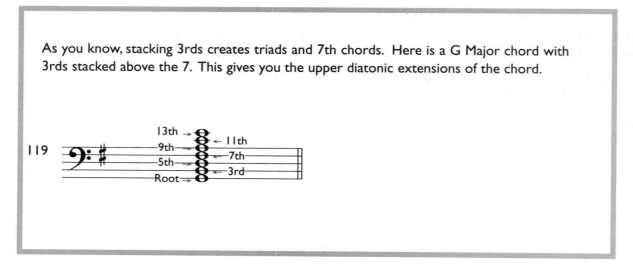

Not all diatonic extensions work on every chord. Some are "avoid" notes and will not sound good. Virtually any note can be added to dominant 7 chords, while extensions to major and minor chords will be more limited.

COMMON CHORD EXTENSIONS AND ALTERATIONS

Some extensions above certain chords lend themselves to alteration. That means that we can raise them or lower them with accidentals, adding even more tension and interest to the sound. The dominant chord extensions are especially fun. Some examples of altered dominant chords are shown on page 80. Play through them and enjoy the sounds. Then, pick up a good jazz harmony book (try *Theory for the Contemporary Guitarist* by Guy Capuzzo).

Here is a chart to get you started thinking about the possibilities of extensions and altered extensions:

BASIC CHORD	EXTENSIONS
Major 7	9 11 (less common) $\sharp$11 13
Minor 7	9 11 13 $\flat$13 (less common)
Diminished 7	Major 7 9
Minor 7$\flat$5	$\flat$9 9 11 $\flat$13
Dominant 7	$\flat$9 9 $\sharp$9 $\sharp$11 $\flat$13 13

Here are some examples of chord extensions added to a dominant 7 chord with a root of C:

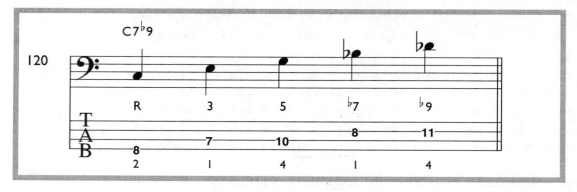

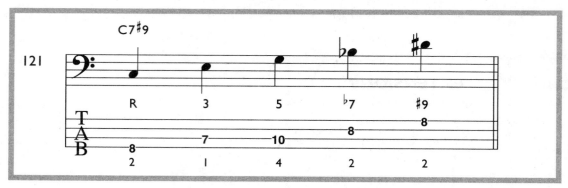

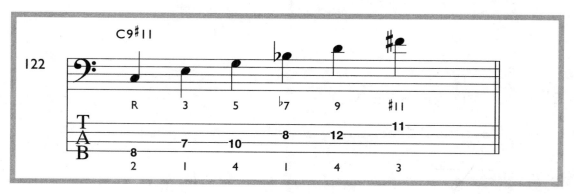

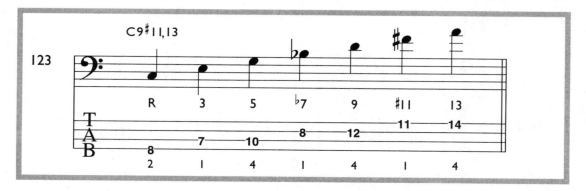

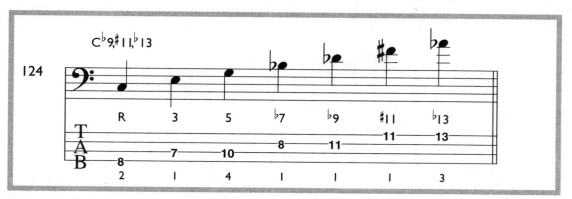

MODES OF THE HARMONIC MINOR SCALE

The modes of the harmonic minor scale produce some very interesting sounds. They are arrived at in exactly the same manner as the modes of the major scale. You can start and end a scale on each note of the harmonic minor scale, and thus create seven different modes of the scale.

Below are the scales built on each of the scale degrees of the C Harmonic Minor scale. These are not the only names used for these modes but these names describe each mode as an alteration of a mode of the major scale—which can make them easier to understand. The chord that corresponds to the scale is also shown. These are not the only fingerings for these modes. Try to invent some fingerings of your own.

The Lydian ♭7 mode, and other altered modes, are often used to solo over dominant 7 chords. These are not the only possible fingerings. Invent some of your own.

SCALE SYLLABUS

The center column lists some of the scales that you can use to improvise over the chords in the left column. The column on the far right shows the spellings for scales with a C root. Many of the scales are now familiar to you, but some are new. Have fun trying these scales over the chords.

CHORD	SCALE/MODE	THE NOTES IN C
Major Major 7	Major	C D E F G A B C
	Major Pentatonic	C D E G A C
	Lydian	C D E F♯ G A B C
	Bebop Major	C D E F G G♯ A B C
	Lydian Augmented	C D E F♯ G♯ A B C
Dominant 7	Mixolydian	C D E F G A B♭ C
	Major Pentatonic	C D E G A C
	Bebop Dominant	C D E F G A B♭ B C
	Lydian ♭7	C D E F♯ G A B♭ C
	Whole Tone	C D E F♯ G♯ B♭ C
	Half-Step/Whole-Step Diminished	C D♭ D♯ E F♯ G A B♭ C
	Diminished Whole Tone	C D♭ D♯ E F♯ G♯ B♭ C
	Blues Scale	C E♭ F F♯ G B♭ C
Minor Minor 7	Dorian	C D E♭ F G A B♭ C
	Minor Pentatonic	C E♭ F G B♭ C
	Bebop Minor	C D E♭ E F G A B♭ C
	Melodic Minor	C D E♭ F G A B C
	Blues Scale	C E♭ F F♯ G B♭ C
	Harmonic Minor	C D E♭ F G A♭ B C

There are many scale choices for each type of chord. If there are altered tones in the chord you are playing over, that will help you determine which scale to use. For example, if there is a ♯11 in the dominant chord, the Lydian ♭7 is a good choice, because it has the ♭7 that all dominant chords have, and the ♯4, which is the same as a ♯11.

Here's another example:
C7♯9—Even though the Mixolydian and Lydian ♭7 scales both can be used to play over a dominant 7 chord, you would probably want to use the diminished whole tone or the half-step/whole-step diminished scale, both of which contain the ♯9 tone.

Here are three different approaches when soloing over chord changes:

1) **Chordal:** Using mostly chord tones and chord extensions (arpeggios) for your solo.

2) **Scales:** A. Using a single scale to play over many chords.
   B. Using a different scale for each chord ("blowing over the changes").

3) **Melodies:** Try to create a melody over the chord progression. (This leads to a more lyrical style of playing and actually could be the most challenging.)

Below is a solo primarily using arpeggios to play over the chords. Notice the use of chord extensions. In some places, passing tones are used to connect chord tones, as in bar 10.

ARPEGGIO SOLO

Track 96

MODAL TUNES

The 1940s and '50s were the *bebop* era of jazz. In bebop, pioneered by Charlie Parker, Dizzy Gillespie and Bud Powell, many notes were used in the solos including chord extensions, and a lot of chromaticism. These players had a lot of "chops," which allowed them to play tunes at extremely fast tempos. In the 1960s, Miles Davis and Gerry Mulligan, among others, developed *cool jazz*. In this style, improvisations were more laid back, tempos were not as fast and improvisations were less busy. Then, Miles Davis once again helped pioneer another style of jazz called *modal jazz*. In modal jazz, a single chord can last for eight to sixteen bars or longer, giving the improviser lots of time to explore each chord. Players improvised over the chord thinking of a scale and not just chord tones.

In the next example, a Dmin7 chord lasts for eight bars. When you look at the Scale Syllabus on page 83, you will see that the Dorian mode is a good scale choice over a minor chord. The notes used in this eight-bar solo are all from the D Dorian mode.

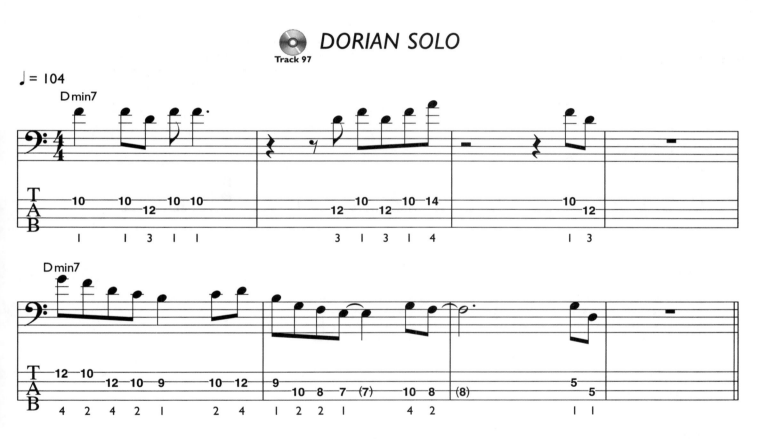

DORIAN SOLO
Track 97

Checkout modal tunes such as *So What* by Miles Davis and *Impressions* by John Coltrane. That will give you a good idea of what the possibilities are. There are tons of books about how scales are used to solo over chords such as *The Chord and Scale Finder* and the *Guitar Mode Encyclopedia*, both by Jody Fisher.

Playing Chords and Harmonics

CHORDS

One of the techniques many bassists are using to expand the role of the bass is playing chords. It is not unusual to hear a bassist use chords to *comp* (accompany) behind a guitar solo. Bassists have been playing 5ths on the bass for a long time, but now you hear many bassists playing triads and 7 chords.

Here are fingerings for major triads, minor triads and three types of 7 chords. Some fingerings may be more practical than others. Try them all and you can decide what works for you. The roots are shown in gray. Play only those strings with fingerings. There are no open strings in these chords, so you can move them anywhere on the neck.

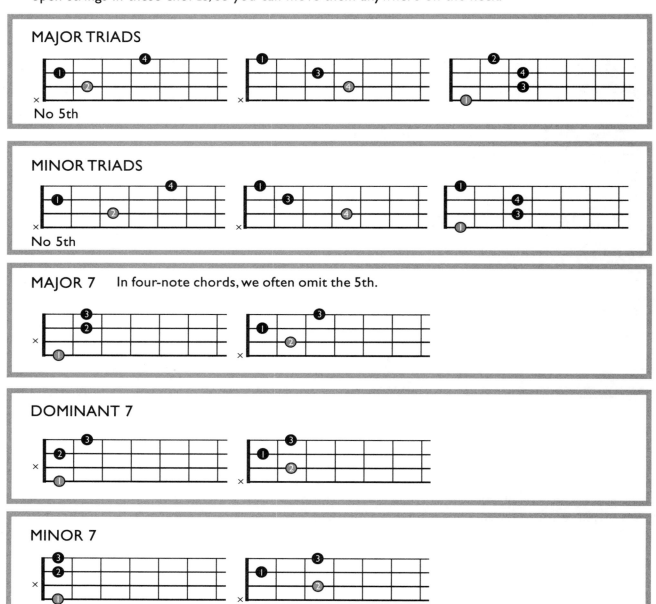

MAJOR TRIADS

No 5th

MINOR TRIADS

No 5th

MAJOR 7   In four-note chords, we often omit the 5th.

DOMINANT 7

MINOR 7

Below is a twelve-bar blues that will help you with your chord playing. Notice the use of the double-stop technique introduced on page 70. Also notice that the music is written in two *voices* (parts). In each measure, the notes with the stems down add up to four beats, and the notes with the stems up (plus the rests) add up to four beats. There are not eight beats in each measure. Think of it as being two parts written on one staff. Use your right thumb to play the notes with the stems down, and your 1st and 2nd fingers to play the notes with the stems up.

Here is a solo tune for you to play that uses a variety of chord types. The first chord in the tune, F/C, is a slash chord. Remember, the character to the left of the slash is the chord. The character to the right of the slash is the lowest note. Slash chords are handy when the bass note is something other than the root, or even a non-chord tone.

This tune has lots of syncopation between the upper and lower parts. Count and clap the parts separately, then put them together. Take your time and have fun!

8va = Play an octave higher than written

CHORD TUNE

Track 99

D.C. a Coda = *Da Capo al Coda*. Return to the beginning and play up to the coda sign ✛.
Then, skip to the end and play the Coda (ending).

HARMONICS

Playing *harmonics* is another technique that has helped bassists expand the role of their instrument. Harmonics are very pure, chime-like sounds. Bassists such as Jaco Pastorius, Michael Manring and Victor Wooten have explored harmonics and used them frequently. Pastorius' *Portrait of Tracy* was the tune that first made people aware of the vast possibilities of harmonics on the bass.

You should pick up a good theory book and also do some reading about the physics of acoustics to learn a bit about the musical and scientific concepts behind the *overtone series* and playing harmonics. Briefly, think of each musical note as being a lot like light in a prism. A prism can show how a single beam of light contains a rainbow of different colors. Likewise, each musical note actually contains an array of higher pitches, called *overtones* or *harmonics*, above the *fundamental tone* you are playing. Playing harmonics is like separating out one of the colors in the prism—we play a specific overtone. This chapter will introduce you to playing single harmonics and show you the location of the first seven harmonics.

HARMONICS OF THE 1ST STRING

Pluck the open 1st string. The note we hear is the fundamental tone. There is a simple technique we can use to hear the overtones.

Lightly touch the 1st string (G) directly above the 12th fret. You must place your finger directly over the fret-wire, otherwise the harmonic will not sound. Don't push the string down to the fretboard; rather, while your finger is lightly touching the string over the 12th fret, pluck the string with your right hand. You should hear a chime-like sound that is one octave higher than the open string.

The point on which you place your finger to produce the harmonic is called a *node*. When playing harmonics, it is helpful to pull your finger away from the node as quickly as possible after plucking the string. This prevents you from interfering with the vibration of the string.

The harmonic at the 12th fret is the 1st harmonic. The 2nd harmonic, an octave plus a 5th above the fundamental tone, is located over the 7th fret and is played using the same technique. The 3rd harmonic, two octaves above the fundamental tone, is over the 5th fret. The diagrams on pages 91 and 92 show the locations of all the harmonics on the open strings. The 4th and 5th harmonics are a little trickier to play, because they are both located near frets, but not directly on them (see the diagrams). The same goes for the 6th and 7th harmonics. Some harmonics are just below or just above a fret. For example, there's a harmonic just below the 4th fret (4-), and another just above the 3rd (3+).

The table below shows the pitch of the first seven harmonics on the 1st string (G).

HARMONICS ABOVE THE 1ST STRING (G) FUNDAMENTAL TONE

HARMONIC	PITCH	FRET	INTERVAL ABOVE FUNDAMENTAL
1st	G	12	One octave
2nd	D	7	One octave plus a perfect 5th
3rd	G	5	Two octaves
4th	B	4-	Two octaves plus a major 3rd
5th	D	3+	Two octaves plus a perfect 5th
6th	F	3-	Two octaves plus a minor 7 (♭7)
7th	G	2+	Three octaves

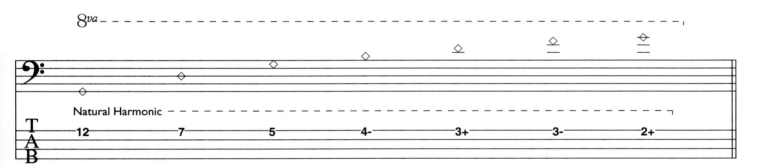

Here is a fretboard diagram that shows the node location and pitch of the first seven harmonics on all four strings of the bass:

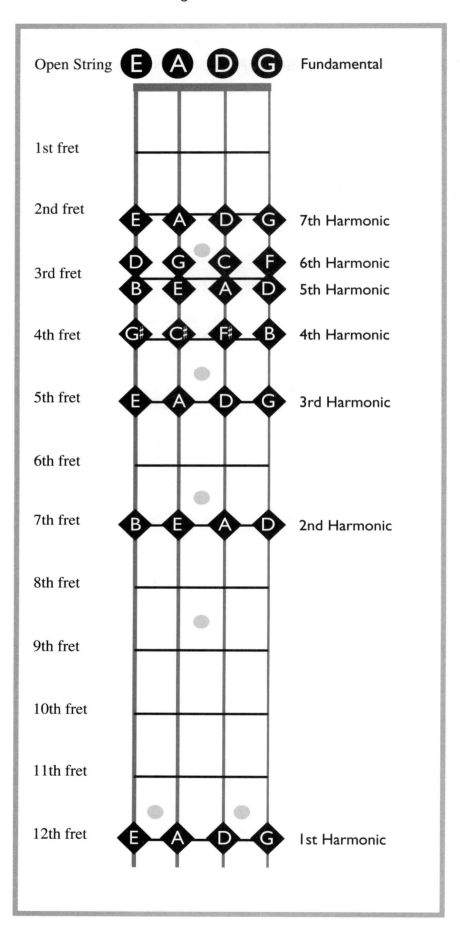

CHAPTER 10

Practicing

Although it is important to spend a lot of time practicing your instrument, it is more important to practice constructively with the time you do have. If you become a professional, you will find that once you start playing gigs night after night, along with rehearsals, writing, teaching, and other activities, practice time is not as plentiful as it was when you first started playing. If you play strictly for fun, you probably have a busy life in your profession or in school. When you have the time to practice, you should make the most of it.

Try to divide your practice time into sections. Let's say you have an hour to practice on a given day. Divide up this time to accomplish several different goals. For example, take 20 minutes practicing scales (major, minor, harmonic minor, melodic minor). There are more scales, as you know, but those should keep you busy. The next 20 minutes can be used to practice arpeggios (major, minor, diminished, augmented, major 7, minor 7, dominant 7, minor7♭5, diminished 7, etc.). The last 20 minutes of the one-hour practice session can be used to work on a tune (learn the chords, work on creating bass lines for the chords, practice improvising over the changes). If you have more than one hour, you can incorporate reading into your practice session. If not, you can alternate what to practice for each session. For example, exclude reading on Monday, exclude scales on Tuesday, and exclude arpeggios on Wednesday. If you can incorporate these suggestions into your practice sessions, you are on your way to improving as a player.

LISTENING

Listening is as important as practicing. Remember, music is a *heard* art. The ears are what it is all about. You can always learn something from listening. This will help you grow as a player and help you learn things that you are not going to get out of a book.

Try to listen to and play with musicians who have more experience and are better than you in some respects. You can also learn from listening to players that are not so good. From them, you can learn what to *not* do. The important thing is to listen to other players as much as possible.

When you do not have the opportunity to listen to other players live, listen to a recording. Listen to what the bass part is doing in the context of the music. Try to figure out the bass line. This is an excellent way to help develop your ears. After you have figured out the bass line, play along with the recording. Playing with a rhythm section that is playing in time will help you develop a good sense of time.

If you're not practicing "in time," it is almost better to not practice at all. Remember, as a bass player, you are responsible for laying down the groove for the band. This does not mean that you cannot do any constructive practicing without a metronome, but using one as often as you can will help you with your time-keeping.

If you can get your hands on one, a drum machine is an interesting alternative to a metronome. Like the metronome, a drum machine helps you practice in time but in a more interesting way, since it can play grooves. You can practice funk grooves, Latin bass lines, walking bass lines and any other bass line you want.

Metronomes and drum machines are great tools for practicing, but whenever you have the opportunity to play with a good drummer, take it. Although technology offers substitutes, there is nothing like interacting with a drummer and feeling the bass lines rumble through your chest.

Practice, practice, practice—and enjoy!

WHAT'S NEXT?

Now that you have completed the *Complete Electric Bass Method*, you might be wondering how you can put the information you have learned to use, or what you can do to learn more. Here are some suggestions:

PLAY WITH OTHER MUSICIANS

Though this method contains vital informationan that can make you a better bassist, there are still lots of things you can do that will contribute to your growth as a musician. Probably the most important of these is playing with other musicians. Although it is important to do, practicing at home with a metronome or a drum machine doesn't let you hear what your bass lines sound like against the chords—playing with other musicians does. Last but not least, playing with other musicians is *fun* and that's what it is all about.

BOOKS

There are lots of books out there. The *Complete Electric Bass Method* contains a wealth of information, but you can choose an area of study that interests you and find books that are devoted to that subject. Many areas of study can help you grow as a bass player, such as music theory, jazz improvisation, sight-reading and Afro-Cuban bass lines, to name a few. Get out to the library, your area music store or on to the Internet and explore the many thousands of publications available on topics of interest to you.

LISTEN TO OTHER PLAYERS

Get out and listen to other musicians as often as you can. Hanging out at jam sessions helps you meet other players and hear what they are doing. If you want your phone to ring for gigs, you want people to notice you, so you should be out there playing and being part of the music scene in your area. If you sit at home all the time, no one will know what a great player you are!

Keep Playin'!